GHOST TOWNS

BODIE, CALIFORNIA

Ben Nussbaum

Consultant
Jamey Acosta, M.S.Ed.
Reading Specialist and English Learner TOSA

Publishing Credits
Rachelle Cracchiolo, M.S.Ed., *Publisher*
Emily R. Smith, M.A.Ed., *SVP of Content Development*
Véronique Bos, *VP of Creative*
Dona Herweck Rice, *Senior Content Manager*
Fabiola Sepulveda, *Art Director*

Image Credits: p.4 California State University, Chico, Meriam Library SpecialCollections; p.6 Alamy/EThamPhoto; p.8 Alamy (top)/Russ Bishop; p.9 Alamy/Penta Springs Limited; pp.10–11 Courtesy of the California History Room, California State Library, Sacramento, California; p.15 Courtesy of the California History Room, California State Library, Sacramento, California; p.20 California State University, Chico, Meriam Library SpecialCollections; p.21 (top) Alamy; p.21(bottom) Alamy/Allstar Picture Library Ltd.; p.29 Alamy/peace portal photo; p.29 Alamy (top)/Old Paper Studios (bottom); all other images from iStock or Shutterstock

Library of Congress Cataloging-in-Publication Data
Names: Nussbaum, Ben, 1975- author.
Title: Ghost towns: Bodie, California / Ben Nussbaum.
Description: Huntington Beach, CA : Teacher Created Materials, [2025] | Title from ECIP cover. | Audience: Ages 7-12 | Summary: "When miners found a rich deposit of gold in Bodie, people from all around rushed to the town. Bodie was an exciting and dangerous place to live. People in Bodie saw explosions and gunfights-and gold! But today, Bodie is empty. It has become a famous ghost town"-- Provided by publisher.
Identifiers: LCCN 2024039516 (print) | LCCN 2024039517 (ebook) | ISBN 9781644910016 (paperback) | ISBN 9781644910344 (ebook)
Subjects: LCSH: Ghost towns--California--Juvenile literature. | Frontier and pioneer life--California--Bodie--Juvenile literature. | Bodie (Calif.)--Gold discoveries--Juvenile literature. | Bodie (Calif.)--History--Juvenile literature.
Classification: LCC F869.B65 N87 2025 (print) | LCC F869.B65 (ebook) | DDC 979.448--dcundefined
LC record available at https://lccn.loc.gov/2024039516
LC ebook record available at https://lccn.loc.gov/2024039517

This book may not be reproduced or distributed in any way without prior written consent from the publisher.

TCM | Teacher Created Materials

5482 Argosy Avenue
Huntington Beach, CA 92649
www.tcmpub.com
ISBN 978-1-6449-1001-6
© 2025 Teacher Created Materials, Inc.

Table of Contents

No Place Like Bodie 4

The Wildest Years 6

Bullets and Blizzards 12

From Gold Town to Ghost Town 16

Saving Bodie 22

Tourists and Ghosts 26

Imagine It! 28

Glossary 30

Index 31

Your Turn! 32

No Place Like Bodie

Once upon a time, people rushed to Bodie, California, hoping to get rich. They came on foot, in wagons, or by horse or mule. Wagons pulled into town. They brought supplies, people looking for work, and miners looking for gold. Speedy stagecoaches carried gold out of town. Guards with shotguns kept watch for robbers.

Visitors to Bodie saw a city alive with activity. They may have seen a gunfight, a wrestling match, or a huge parade. Anything could have happened there!

Bodie's Main Street stretched for a mile. It was full of places to eat, rest, dance, and celebrate. Miners visiting the **saloon** sometimes paid for drinks with gold dust.

A large building on a nearby hill made a rumbling noise throughout the day. Here, machines tore apart rocks so workers could grab little bits of the precious gold threaded through them.

freight team at Bodie, California, around 1880

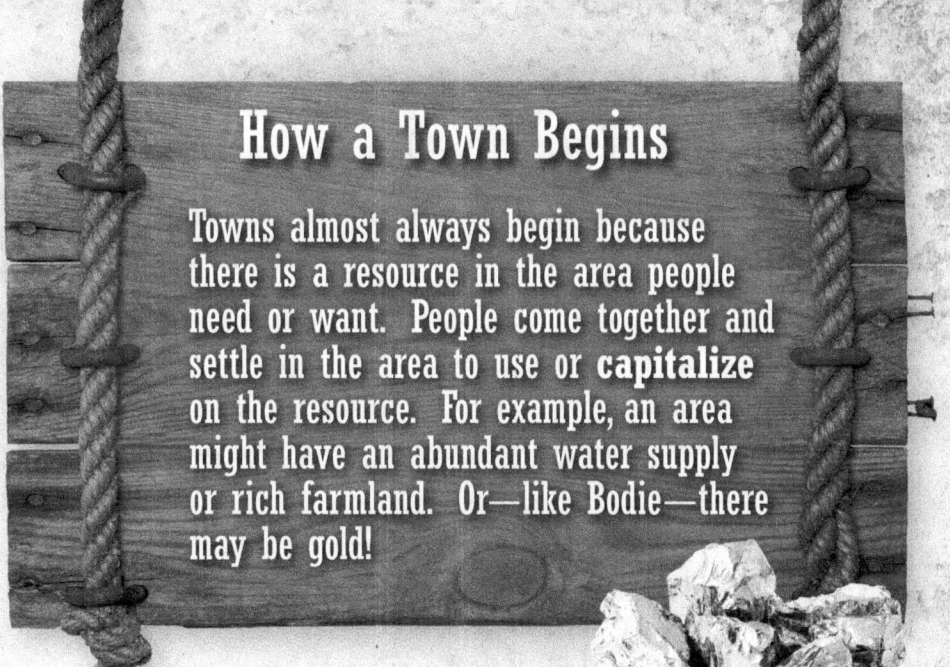

How a Town Begins

Towns almost always begin because there is a resource in the area people need or want. People come together and settle in the area to use or **capitalize** on the resource. For example, an area might have an abundant water supply or rich farmland. Or—like Bodie—there may be gold!

Today, the rumble is silent. The streets of Bodie are quiet. Empty houses shake in the wind. Bodie is a ghost town. The buildings still stand, but no one lives there anymore.

Main Street, Bodie today

The Wildest Years

In 1859, a **prospector** found small amounts of gold where Bodie would soon develop. Word of this success started to spread. A few people came to the area to dig mines, hoping to find even more gold.

But this small amount of gold did not create a **boom**. Bodie grew slowly. At first, only a few dozen people lived there. Then a hundred. Then a few hundred. Things changed rapidly in 1876. That is when a huge streak of gold was discovered in one of the mines. Suddenly, a **gold rush** was on! Word spread rapidly, and soon more than 10,000 people lived in Bodie.

Miners poured into town, hoping to make a fortune. Carpenters, painters, shopkeepers, and many others came as well, hoping to work. But, no one wanted only to work. They wanted ways to have fun as well. In Bodie, they found many options for entertainment. People could watch a boxing match or a horse race. They could attend a play or a show. They could spend all day playing card games in saloons.

Bodie's saloon

Body, Bodey, Bodie

Bodie was named for the man who first found gold there. His first name was either William or Waterman. His last name was either Body or Bodey. According to legend, a sign painter changed the spelling of the town to Bodie because he thought it looked better.

Miners like these ones flocked to Bodie, California.

Many people in Bodie joined **fraternal** organizations. These groups were like clubs. They each hosted a Grand Ball once a year. At the balls, women and men wore their fanciest clothes. They danced for hours. At midnight, they went to a fine supper at a hotel.

The Dechambeau Hotel (left) hosted many balls and parties.

Horses and wagons were the main form of transportation in Bodie.

Cornish Wrestling

Many miners were from Cornwall, England. This area has its own style of wrestling. The wrestlers wear heavy jackets. They try to grab the other person's jacket and throw them to the ground. Cornish wrestling was a part of many festivities in Bodie.

A number of people who lived in Bodie were from China. There was even a whole part of Bodie called Chinatown. Chinese New Year was a big event there. Every winter, there were three days of "gongs, drums, bombs, and firecrackers," according to a Bodie newspaper.

The Fourth of July, celebrating U.S. independence, was the grandest celebration of the year in Bodie. It was a patriotic festival, filled with food, fun, and lots of red, white, and blue. Buildings were decorated with flags. And while no trees grew in Bodie (it sat above the **timber line**), the town was filled with trees for the celebration. On the Fourth of July, people carted trees into town for decoration. They put them in buckets, lining Main Street with them. The trees were **festive**, and they added to the celebration.

In the morning on the Fourth of July, a big parade marched through town. Each club in town marched in the parade, and so did military veterans. Bands and drummers marched, too. The whole town took part.

The afternoon was all about contests. People raced, wrestled, and played tug-of-war. Baseball teams representing different mines played against each other. At night, the Miner's Union held a huge ball. This group had its own building on Main Street.

stagecoaches in front of the Grand Central Hotel in Bodie, California, 1880

Even on days that were not holidays, the Miner's Union Hall was the center of life in Bodie. Here, people could cheer at a boxing match. They could attend a church service. They could watch a play. In fact, they could do all this in the same weekend!

Ella M. Cain was born in Bodie and spent time there as a child before moving to Bridgeport, about 19 miles (31 kilometers) away. She returned as an adult and become a schoolteacher there. She then wrote a book about Bodie. She wrote that in Bodie, "the sky was the limit." Its best years were "the wildest, maddest years the West has ever known."

The Miner's Union Hall is now a museum.

Bullets and Blizzards

Bodie could be exciting and fun, but it was not an easy place to live.

Gunfights sometimes broke out in Bodie. In one fight, people battled over who had the right to mine a certain piece of land. One group said they owned it, and another group argued that they did. Before long, bullets flew back and forth, and two people died.

All that possible gold brought some people to Bodie who wanted an easy way to get rich, and they did not want to work for it. Some people just wanted to be part of the excitement. Some people wanted to steal. People did not always honor the law. Crime was common, and the use of opium (an illegal drug) was high.

Around the country, Bodie became famous for its **lawlessness**. An expression became popular, far beyond Bodie's borders. People referred to the "Bad Man from Bodie." This phrase did not refer to a particular person. It meant any rough, violent man.

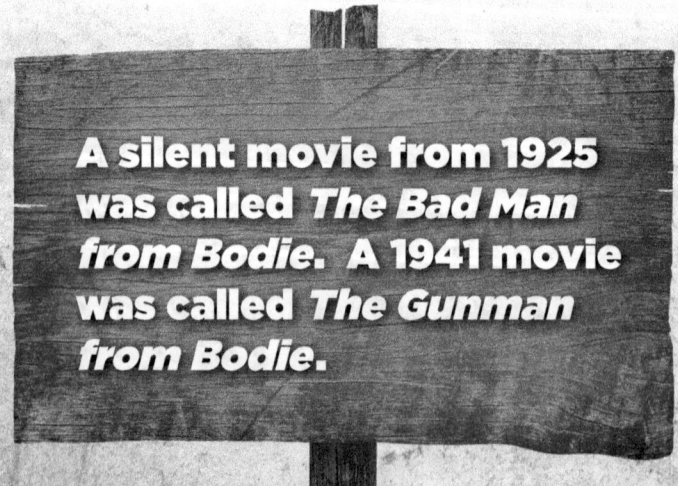

A silent movie from 1925 was called *The Bad Man from Bodie*. A 1941 movie was called *The Gunman from Bodie*.

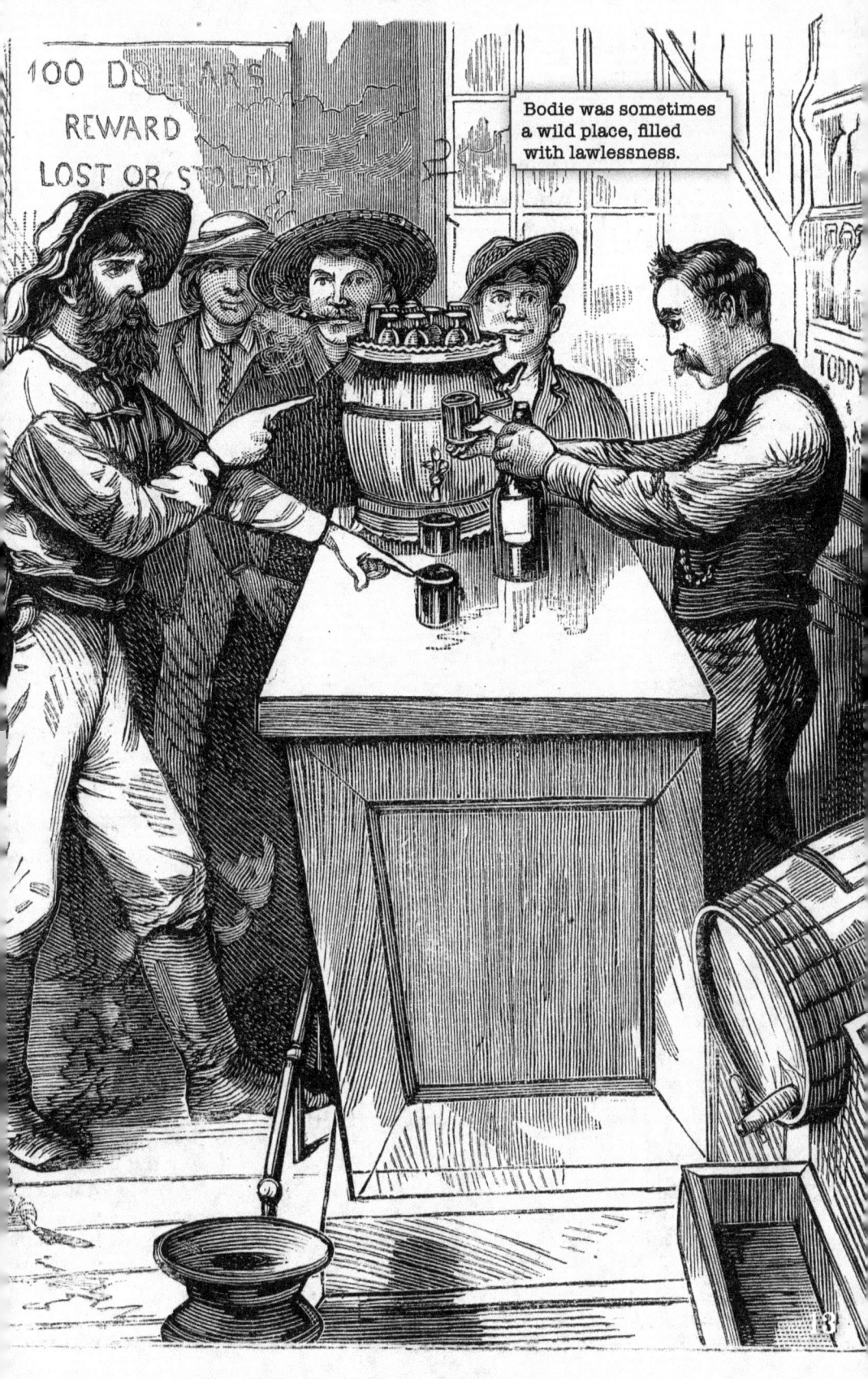

As the gold rush settled, Bodie began to calm down. More families moved in, and two churches were built. Things became quieter and much more like a typical town. People lived, worked, and raised their children. Gunfights were not so common.

In fact, blizzards became a much bigger problem than bullets.

Bodie sits high in the mountains. Even in the summer, the temperature often drops below freezing. In the winter, the days can be **frigid**, and the nights are worse. Very strong winds are common in Bodie, too.

Snow Explosion

Sometimes, the snow was so thick in Bodie that people did not shovel it. Instead, they exploded it away. They used bombs that were made to clear away rocks in the mines.

The first winter after the gold rush dimmed was even colder than normal. People huddled inside small, **drafty** houses. Their fires were often very small because wood was **scarce** in Bodie. Many people died that winter because of the cold. Their bodies had to be pulled to the cemetery on a sled across the frozen ground.

Even today, it is very hard to get to Bodie in the winter. The roads are blocked by snow. Some people ski in just to see the town.

Reading Store snowed in at Bodie, California, 1911

From Gold Town to Ghost Town

Bodie did not become a ghost town overnight. It had many ups and downs along the way. There were hard times and good times alike.

Only a few years after the huge **deposit** of gold was discovered, some of the mines closed. It didn't make sense to keep their businesses going without making much money. These mines could not pay their workers simply on the hope of finding more gold. When their mines closed, some workers had to leave Bodie to find jobs in other places.

And then there was the fire. In 1892, a huge fire roared through Bodie. It started in a bakery in the middle of the night. The fire spread quickly and destroyed most of Main Street.

In its prime, Bodie had about 2,000 structures.

The people of Bodie were **resilient**, and they rebuilt Main Street. They did so by moving buildings from other parts of town. But Bodie was never as big as it had been, and it did not **flourish** as it once did.

Some events helped spark some life into Bodie. For example, electricity came to Bodie the year after the big fire. Mines did not have to use steam power anymore, and that helped things run more easily. Other tools and inventions gave the miners new ways to find gold as well.

modern photo of Main Street, Bodie as a ghost town

Still, there was no way to put gold back in the ground. Every day, less gold remained under Bodie. That meant less success for miners.

As people left Bodie, empty buildings became common around town. And in 1915, the last big mine closed. A couple of years later, the railroad that went to Bodie shut down. The tracks were torn up, and the metal was used in other places. Then, the electric line that ran to Bodie was shut down. Everything that made the town prosper left piece by piece.

A few **hardy** people stayed in town, and they mined a lot like the first settlers in Bodie had done. But, it was exhausting work. By 1920, the whole town of Bodie had only about 100 people left in it. It also had more than 100 empty buildings. Bodie felt like a ghost town, even though some people still lived there.

But then, suddenly, Bodie got a surprise second chance.

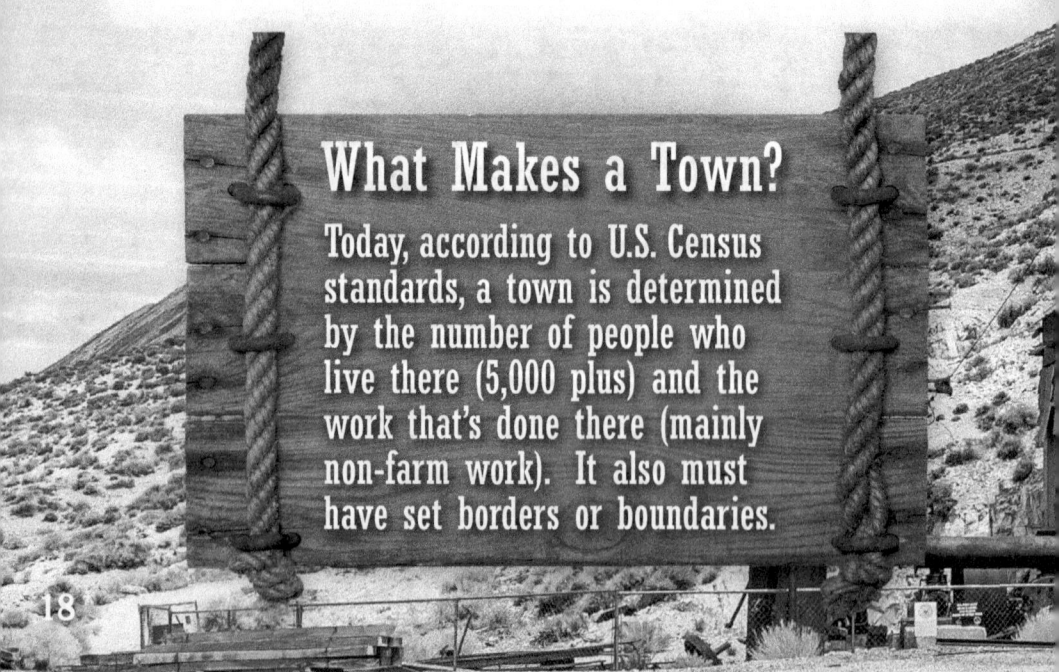

What Makes a Town?
Today, according to U.S. Census standards, a town is determined by the number of people who live there (5,000 plus) and the work that's done there (mainly non-farm work). It also must have set borders or boundaries.

one of Bodie's old mines

Bodie had another boom. Companies came to town to try to find gold even deeper underground. Electricity was brought back to Bodie. Stores and restaurants opened. The school was given a fresh coat of paint. Cars chugged down Main Street. Bodie even opened a gas station. The town appeared to be on the rise again.

But, the new companies could not find any more rich deposits of gold. After just a couple years, they gave up. And in 1932, a terrible fire ignited once again. It ripped through town and destroyed most of the grand buildings left in Bodie.

With the town weak and failing, the last mine closed in 1942. By this time, the United States had entered World War II. People throughout the country had to focus on helping the war efforts. They were not allowed to mine for gold, which was not needed for the war.

When the war was over, some people came back to Bodie. They opened a mining plant. But one last fire came to Bodie. It destroyed the plant. All hope for renewal was lost. The last of Bodie's residents left. Now, Bodie really was a ghost town.

the Mono County Bank, 1880

Hell's Heroes

A movie from 1930 called *Hell's Heroes* was shot in Bodie. It is a great record of what Bodie looked like before the 1932 fire.

Hell's Heroes movie

Saving Bodie

As people were leaving Bodie, one family bought more and more of its land: the Cain family.

In Bodie's best years, the Cains owned many businesses. They believed another gold rush would come to Bodie. They pictured a day when the streets would be full of people. So, as Bodie emptied, they hired someone to live in Bodie and protect it. This person became Bodie's **caretaker**.

schoolhouse

For Memory's Sake

Ella M. Cain gathered information about Bodie by interviewing its oldest residents. She kept a notepad and pen with her most of the time to write their stories.

Ella M. Cain, the teacher who wrote a book about Bodie, also played a big role in saving the town. Sometimes, she went to Bodie to give the caretaker a day off. She sat in the old school. If people came in, she would tell them all about Bodie.

More people started going to Bodie just to see the empty town. This gave the Cains an idea. Maybe the town could be saved just the way it was. Maybe Bodie should stay a ghost town.

Generations of the Cains watched over Bodie for many years. In 1962, they decided Bodie should belong to everyone. They gave their part of the town to the state of California. A couple years later, hundreds of people came to Bodie to celebrate it becoming an official California State Park. People gave speeches, and a band entertained the crowd. Children laughed and played while adults toured the town. On that day, Bodie did not feel like a ghost town.

Since then, the park has grown in size. Now, the state of California owns all of Bodie. **Rangers** at the park tell visitors about the town and its history. They give tours and make sure no one is damaging anything or taking things from Bodie. Some rangers live in Bodie, even in the winter. That way, Bodie is protected all the time.

Bad Luck Bodie

Visitors to Bodie are not allowed to take anything from the town. A ranger invented a story that people who did would have bad luck. Some people return items they took by sending them back in the mail. They are afraid and don't want bad luck!

Tourists and Ghosts

About 200,000 people come to Bodie each year. They walk down Main Street, looking through windows and taking pictures. They imagine what it was like to live in Bodie in its prime. They look for clues about the people who once lived there and what the town was like when it was bustling with life and activity.

The park department keeps Bodie looking like a ghost town. If a building is about to fall down, rangers prop it up. But they don't paint, fix, or repair anything. They let Bodie wear away naturally.

a Bodie home interior today

In total, about 34 million dollars in gold and silver were mined in Bodie.

a Bodie bedroom today

A few years ago, a company wanted to mine for gold near Bodie. The mining may have destroyed the ghost town. People fought the company, and now it is against the law to mine near Bodie.

There is still some gold under Bodie. For now, it is safe where it is and will stay there for a long time. Bodie's history and memories are safe, too.

Eventually the old western buildings will crumble and turn to dust, and all signs of Bodie will disappear. But that is still a long time away. Until that day, Bodie will remain the famous ghost town it is.

The Bodie Boone Store and Warehouse is no longer open.

Imagine It!

Ella M. Cain was a teacher in Bodie. After it became a ghost town, she would often sit in the old schoolhouse and tell visitors about being a teacher there.

Even today, the schoolhouse in Bodie still has old things the teachers and students used. These books, toys, and games tell a story about Bodie and the people who lived there.

Think about a modern classroom. Imagine what it would look like if it were part of a ghost town. Then, complete the following:

1. Select five things that are part of a modern classroom.

2. Imagine that someone 100 years from now is looking at these objects. What do you want them to know about the objects? Write a few sentences about each one.

3. Pretend that it is many years from now. You have to explain what school was like when you were young. Using the objects you chose, explain a typical day in school.

Bodie schoolhouse

All students in Bodie met in the same classroom with one teacher, like this class does.

Glossary

boom—a sudden and large growth spurt or expansion

capitalize—make money from

caretaker—someone who takes care of something or someone else

deposit—an amount of something valuable that is left in one place

drafty—cold, with the wind coming in through the walls

festive—happy and exciting, filled with celebration

flourish—to do well or be successful

fraternal—something similar or related to brothers

frigid—very cold

gold rush—a brief period of time when people rush to a new source of gold

hardy—tough, able to endure pain

lawlessness—the lack of good police

prospector—someone who travels around looking for gold

rangers—people who work for a park

resilient—able to become strong or healthy again after something bad happens

saloon—a type of bar or restaurant

scarce—rare, hard to find

timber line—an imaginary line on a mountain or high elevation that marks the level above which no trees grow

Index

"Bad Man from Bodie," 12

Bodey, William, 7

Cain, Ella M., 11, 23

Cain family, 22–24

California State Park, 24

Chinatown, 9

Cornwall, England, 9

electricity, 17, 20

fire, 15–17, 20–21

Fourth of July, 9–10

Miner's Union Hall, 11

trees, 9

winter, 9, 14–15, 24

Your Turn!

You can have some fun making a before-and-after ghost-town model. Here's how:

1. Find a picture of a building from the late 1800s to early 1900s. It can be a house, shop, bank, hotel, train depot—anything.

2. Gather materials to make your building models. These might be construction paper, poster board, balsa wood, scissors, tape, glue, markers, paint, etc.

3. Using the photo as a guide, make a 3D model of the building. Be as detailed as you can be.

4. Make a second model of the building, but this one showing the building as sitting empty for many years. How might time and disuse have changed the structure?